ENTREPRENEURSHIP
&
THE ENTREPRENEURIAL
JOURNEY

To Graeme

Thankyou
fr ya Suppot
fraser.

Fraser J. Hay

Copyright Notice

© Fraser J. Hay, 2018

Introduction

The best start-up advice anyone could receive comes from an unlikely source:

"Let me tell you something you already know. The world ain't all sunshine and rainbows. It's a very mean and nasty place and I don't care how tough you are it will beat you to your knees and keep you there permanently if you let it. You, me, or nobody is gonna hit as hard as life. But it ain't about how hard ya hit. It's about how hard you can get hit and keep moving forward. How much you can take and keep moving forward. That's how winning is done!"

- ***Sylvestor Stallone in the film "Rocky Balboa"***

It's so true.

Far too many books, TV celebrities, Success Coaches and Internet Marketing Gurus are often unrealistic in the way they explain starting and growing a business for readers, delegates, subscribers and viewers. Many are persuaded, even fooled into thinking it's all going to be very simple, easy and straight forward, but believe me it's not.

Your entrepreneurial journey can be very emotional, stressful and you will get frustrated, angry and encounter many disappointments along the way. You will also experience amazing times en route to your success accompanied by great feelings of fulfillment and achievement. The simple reason is that we experience, we learn, we evolve and our business grows too as we continue to apply the learning from the lessons learned.

Unlike the classrooms of the many business schools around the globe, with your entrepreneurial journey and your business, the tests come first then the lessons are learned.

You will also experience personal, professional and commercial growth. Real growth.

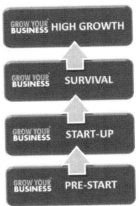

There will be many issues, challenges and obstacles to identify, address and overcome for each stage of your entrepreneurial journey, and with this book I want to pre-empt some of them, in fact over **999** of them and get you, your team and your family thinking and taking action.

This book will help you to get clarity, vision and purpose about –

1. The reasons and concerns you have about starting a business.
2. Documenting your model, vision and strategy.
3. How you will generate exposure, leads, sales & referrals.
4. What your growth plans are as you scale, grow or even exit.

You can also keep returning and referring to the book as you and your business continue to grow and overcome the challenges in each stage of your journey. The purpose of the book is to get you thinking, prioritising and taking responsibility and action to achieve your entrepreneurial goals.

There are NO answers in this book, but there are many different questions to get you thinking and empower you to action in

wanting to progress to the next stage of your entrepreneurial journey. After all, no one knows your business or idea better than you.

There is quite a focus on marketing throughout the book as you encounter many different challenges at the different stages of growth as you pursue starting and growing your business.

After all, marketing is the lifeblood of any business, and the more customers you have, ideally the quicker and faster you will grow, but that too can also present its own set of challenges.

Sometimes the same lessons are repeated until we learn from them and apply the learning. Some questions are repeated in the book to remind you to prioritise and empower you to action.

In fact, there are very specific entrepreneurial issues, challenges and obstacles that maybe holding you back and preventing you from achieving the real results you want on the current stage of your entrepreneurial journey and with this book I want to highlight as many of them as I can.

 When you see this symbol throughout the book. Pause & Reflect. Make notes, Answer the Question or Complete the exercise. This will greatly assist you.

Just reading and reflecting on the content will have little effect on the results you can and should be generating until you convert these "thoughts" into action. Sorry, but it's true. I can lead a horse to water, but I can't make it drink. However, if you need or want help then just ask.

It's your business. You're in control. You make the decisions. Decide to take responsibility and action today. Start experiencing the breakthroughs and results you and your stakeholders want.

Ready to start and grow your business? If so, then you just don't know how big it could get...

Fraser J. Hay
February, 2018

Table of Contents

Part 1 - Pre-Start

At a crossroads?

Identify the issues, challenges and obstacles that are holding you back and preventing you from achieving the goals you want in life. Answer each of the questions below, then complete the exercise at the end of the section.

Do you feel valued, appreciated and compensated for what you do at work?

Do you know your true debt position, how much you really owe and to whom?

Do you know your true net worth and have you prepared a net worth statement?

Do you feel great about yourself and your current circumstances?

Do you have clarity on what you feel, think and want?

Are you able to say "NO" firmly and politely to family/friends without feeling guilty?

Do you know what the meaning of life is (for you)?

Do you know what's holding you back and preventing you from achieving your goals?

Do you have a plan for discovering and living your life's purpose?

Have you written a life plan or personal development plan?

Are your mental, physical, spiritual, career, lifestyle & financial goals clearly defined?

Do you have a means of measuring your progress as you work towards those goals?

Are you on good speaking terms/in harmony with all members of your family?

Can you identify what's annoying, frustrating, or stressing you at the moment?

Are you in mental, physical and spiritual harmony with your life partner?

Do you know what blocks, or beliefs are preventing you from achieving your goals?

Do you have a method, plan or process for dealing with obstacles and challenges?

Do you know what your "intellectual capital" is really worth?

Do you have adequate time & "know how" to explore the "real you"?

Do you have multiple passive income streams not derived from property or the stock market?

Are you receiving the income you want and living the lifestyle you want?

Do you "listen" to your body and what it tells you in terms of discomfort and pain?

Do you know which parts of your body are hurting/aching or are in pain?

Do you know why you are experiencing the discomfort or pain that you are in?

Is your home and workplace free from clutter?

Do you find yourself making excuses why you can't or don't want to complete specific tasks?

Do you know where you want to be in 1, 3 or 5 years time?

Do you know what would make the biggest difference in your life?

For your life to change for the better, do you know what changes you need to make?

Do you tend to worry and get stressed easily when things don't go accordingly to plan?

Do you have a retirement plan & fund in place for when you choose to stop working?

Are you in the same or better shape of health & well-being than you were 12 months ago?

Is your home or car free from requiring repair or overdue maintenance?

Do you wish things to continue the way they are at the moment?

Do you want next year to be the same as last year & facing the same challenges?

Do you want more confidence, progress and results in your life and business?

Add up all your NO responses & make a note of your TOTAL
Which of the following best describes your current situation

1. Yes. I'm all fine thanks.
2. Ah, raised some good points. Got me thinking.
3. Woa. I recognise I need to take action at some point.
4. This is all too overwhelming. I need help with this – fast.
5. I'm going to focus on my top 3 priorities from the list.

Your Fears

Identify the issues, challenges and obstacles that are holding you back and preventing you from becoming self-employed or starting your own business. Answer each of the questions below, then complete the exercise at the end of the section.

Do you feel overwhelmed about what's all involved in becoming self-employed?

Are You Struggling where to start in becoming self-employed?

Are you still weighing up the Pros and Cons to becoming self-employed?

Are You Struggling to justify the experience you have, and whether people will buy it?

Are You Struggling to justify the skills you have, and whether people will buy it?

Are You Struggling to justify the knowledge you have, and whether people will buy it?

Are you unsure about working for yourself because you haven't invented anything?

Are you frustrated because you don't have much (or any) start-up capital?

Are you anxious because you haven't protected your idea yet?

Are you unsure what should be included in a business plan?

Are you unsure who to approach other than a bank to get funding or investment?

Are you anxious how you will survive in the early days?

Are you uncertain as to how to find or generate leads for your products or services?

Are you lacking confidence in how to sell, close and covert those leads into sales

Are you frustrated because you haven't fully tested or researched your idea yet?

Are you concerned that you won't get the backup from friends and family that you need?

Are you concerned that you won't get the investment or start-up money you need?

Are you concerned that it might fail, and you will appear foolish to family and friends?

Are you uncertain whether your idea can become a viable business?

Are you anxious whether you'll be able to earn the salary you're currently getting?

Are you worried whether your customers will pay you the prices you feel you're worth?

Do you lack confidence in "selling" your skills, knowledge or talent to strangers?

Are you anxious as to how you'll generate traffic, signups & sales to your website?

Are you unsure whether you can compete against those in the market doing what you do?

Are you concerned that your personal monthly overheads are quite HIGH?

Are you anxious about renting, buying or leasing premises?

Are you worried about finding good quality trustworthy people to work for/help you?

Are you anxious about what's all really needed to make your website work best for you?

Are you concerned about keeping up with all the admin and book keeping?

Are you worried that the business might fail due to lack of demand or working capital?

Are you frustrated that your idea is taking "for ever" to happen & become a reality?

Are you concerned that the only revenue stream you have is just from selling your time?

Are you anxious about public speaking or how to communicate in front of an audience?

Would you consider self-employment if someone else took care of all the book keeping?

Would consider "going it alone" if others were to pay you what you're really worth?

Would you like a FREE Chat to discuss your score and available options?

 Add up all your YES responses & make a note of your TOTAL

Which of the following best describes your current situation

1. Yes. I'm all fine thanks.
2. Ah, raised some good points. Got me thinking.
3. Woa. I recognise I need to take action at some point.
4. This is all too overwhelming. I need help with this – fast.
5. I'm going to focus on my top 3 priorities from the list.

Your Life Purpose

Identify what's missing and preventing you to identify, pursue and achieve your life purpose and the results you want in your life today. Answer each of the questions below, then complete the exercise at the end of the section.

Are you clear on your life purpose?
Do you know how to get clarity on your life purpose?
Are you on your path of discovering your life purpose?

Are you living your life purpose?
Do you know what you need to accomplish your life purpose?
Are you happy with the results you are achieving with your life at the moment?

Do you know what you need to change in order to achieve your life purpose?
Are you willing to make the changes needed to attract what is needed?
Do you know how to manifest the resources you need to complete your life purpose?

Do you have all the resources you need to complete your life purpose?
Do you live your life with integrity by aligning your thoughts, words and actions?
Do you have a life plan?

DO you know where you want to be in 1, 5 and 10 years time?
DO you know what you want to do in 1, 5 and 10 years time?
DO you know what you want to have in 1, 5 and 10 years time?
Do you know what you can offer in order to achieve what you want to be, do & have?
Is your life, home and office clear of "clutter" and piles of "things"?
Do you set clear boundaries with yourself and others?

Do you want to fulfil your life purpose?

Do you have clarity on the results you want to achieve?

Do you need help, guidance and support in creating & executing life strategies?

Do you know what your GIFTS are?

Do you know what your STRENGTHS are?

Do you experience clear inner guidance?

Do you know what's holding you back & preventing you from achieving your purpose?

Is Growth a driving force in your life?

Do you take responsibility for the choices you make and the actions you take?

Do you love the job you do?

Do you believe you have a "mission" to complete?

Could you use a solid, steady, enlightened coach in your corner?

Do you know where you have NOT been successful and why not?

Are you good at "following through" once you make a decision?

Do you give "life" and everything you choose to participate in – 100%?

Do you want help in defining, refining, pursuing or achieving your life purpose?

Do you want next year to be the same as last year & face the same challenges?

Would you like a FREE Chat to discuss your score and available options?

Add up all your NO responses & make a note of your TOTAL
Which of the following best describes your current situation

1. Yes. I'm all fine thanks.
2. **Ah, raised some good points. Got me thinking.**
3. **Woa. I recognise I need to take action at some point.**
4. **This is all too overwhelming. I need help with this – fast.**
5. **I'm going to focus on my top 3 priorities from the list.**

Reasons for Starting a Business

Identify what's holding you back and preventing you from becoming self-employed or starting your own business. Answer each of the questions below, then complete the exercise at the end of the section.

Do you feel undervalued or unappreciated in your current job?
Do you hate your job, boss or the commute to work?
Do you yearn to work for yourself and be your own boss?

Do you want to take control of your life?
Do you want to live your "life purpose"?
Do you yearn for a more rewarding and fulfilling job, role, career or "life"?

Have you been considering working for yourself for 3 months or longer?
Do you have a hobby or passion you'd like to turn into a business?

Have family and friends been encouraging you for a while to go self-employed?

Have you spotted a gap in the market?
Have you invented, created or thought of a NEW original product or service?
Is the timing right for your business idea?

Do you have SKILLS that people want and need and are prepared to pay for?
Do you have KNOWLEDGE that people want and need and are prepared to pay for?
Do you have a TALENT that people want and need and are prepared to pay for?

Do you have personal goals that you'd like to pursue and achieve?

Is it time that you worked for yourself?

Do you want to earn more money than you're earning now?

Do you want more freedom in your life and to be in control of your choices?

Do you want to be rewarded fairly for your time, effort and knowledge?

Do you want to show others that you can achieve something in your life?

Do you feel confident in offering your skills, knowledge or talent for a fee?

Have several people indicated a willingness to buy your idea, product or service?

Do you totally believe in your idea?

Are your personal monthly overheads quite low?

Could you work from home?

Can you deliver your product or service without the need for hiring extra staff?

Do you think your contacts will introduce you to others who need your solution?

Do you think people will pay the fees you want to charge working for yourself?

Do you know how much you need to earn to give you the lifestyle you want?

Do people not only want what you offer, but they NEED it as well?

Will clients and customers recognise the value in what you are proposing to offer?

Can you articulate the problems, pains, needs & concerns you can solve for customers?

Would you consider self-employment if someone else took care of all the book keeping?

Would you consider working for yourself if you knew sales would come in every month?

Would you like a FREE Chat to discuss your score and available options?

Add up all your NO responses & make a note of your TOTAL
Which of the following best describes your current situation

1. Yes. I'm all fine thanks.
2. Ah, raised some good points. Got me thinking.
3. Woa. I recognise I need to take action at some point.
4. This is all too overwhelming. I need help with this – fast.
5. I'm going to focus on my top 3 priorities from the list.

Your Business Idea

Identify what's holding you back and preventing you from becoming self-employed or starting your own business.   Answer each of the questions below, then complete the exercise at the end of the section.

Does your product/service/business serve a presently un-served need?
Does your solution serve an existing market where demand exceeds supply?
Is your solution competitive because of an original & unique commercial advantage?

Have you determined the resources you will need to start up the business?
Have you determined what your "survival" income is for the next 12 months?
Have you determined what your monthly expenses will be for the next 12 months?

Have you protected the name and intellectual property of your business?
Have you decided on the legal structure of your business?
Have you created a Business Start-up Plan & a business plan for your business?

Do you know what/which components should be included in your business plan?
Do you have an exit strategy for your business?
Do you know who your competitors are?

Have you aligned your ideals/values with those of your potential customers?
Are you willing to invest a large amount of your savings to get the

business started?

Have you selected a business location, and lease/rent/freehold mortgage terms?

Do you know the size of your market and whether it's expanding or declining?

Do you know how to raise your visibility, credibility & exposure online & offline?

Do you know how many prospective "customers" there are in your local/national area?

Do you know how many leads you need to give you the revenue you want?

Do you know how much website traffic you need to give you the revenue you want?

Do you know how many referrals do you need to give you the revenue you want?

Do you know what hardware, software, pinkware and netware you require?

Do you know how you will generate traffic and signups via your website?

Can you communicate your idea succinctly, fluently & professionally?

Have you secured the level of investment or funding you require for the business?

Do you have sufficient funds to survive 6 months without income/revenue?

Is there a stunning barrier to entry to stop others copying/executing your idea?

Does your website have an automated lead generation and follow-up process?

Do you know which statutory, mandatory requirements you need to meet?

Do you have your accounting, administration policies, procedures & systems in place?

Have you assembled your team of staff and business advisers?

Have you agreed how they will get compensated, motivated or incentivised?

Have all the necessary legal documentation & agreements been prepared/completed?

Are you satisfied that you have plenty of other revenue streams other than your time?

Would you like online, offline & local help, guidance & support for your business idea?

Would you like a free confidential Chat to discuss your score & your available options?

Add up all your NO responses & make a note of your TOTAL
Which of the following best describes your current situation

1. Yes. I'm all fine thanks.
2. Ah, raised some good points. Got me thinking.
3. Woa. I recognise I need to take action at some point.
4. This is all too overwhelming. I need help with this – fast.
5. I'm going to focus on my top 3 priorities from the list.

Sacrifices You Might Need to Make

Identify what's holding you back and preventing you from becoming self-employed or starting your own business. Answer each of the questions below, then complete the exercise at the end of the section.

Are you prepared to give up a secure income?

Are you prepared to give up short 9am – 5pm (Mon - Fri) Working Days?

Are you prepared to give up a new car this year so you can stay within budget?

Are you prepared to give up some of the luxuries & home comforts you really like?

Are you prepared to give up your foreign holiday this year?

Are you prepared to give up a life of sunshine & rainbows to deal with stressful situations?

Are you prepared to give up family time and put the business first?

Are you prepared to give up sickies and "duvet days"?

Are you prepared to give up relying on other people & to take extra workload on yourself?

Are you prepared to give up free time to learn more and acquire new entrepreneurial skills?

Are you prepared to cut your cloth, save money and stay within your means?

Are you prepared to up your extended lunch break for a quick snack or no lunch at all?

Are you prepared to give up expensive hotel accommodation for cheaper alternatives?

Are you prepared to give up your current salary and taking a drop in wages or earnings?

Are you prepared to give up luxury airlines & travel arrangements for cheaper alternatives?

Are you prepared to give up the work related banter & work in "isolation" from home?

Are you prepared to give up the latest software licences for older or cheaper alternatives?

Are you prepared for having to discount your fees to win the business?

Are you prepared to wait 30 – 45 days (or longer) to get paid for work done?

Are you prepared to fund and finance your business out of your own pocket?

Are you prepared to share the profit in order to get finance or funding?

Are you prepared for doing a lot of admin or financial record keeping?

Are you prepared to give up sick pay when you are unable to work due to illness?

Are you prepared to chase people for money owed?

Are you prepared to use your savings or your partner's savings to get up & running?

Is your partner prepared for you to give up your currently salary & follow your dream?

Is your partner prepared to make the necessary financial sacrifices or cuts?

Are you prepared to give up a quiet work area & work with the kids running around you?

Are you prepared to give up regular funds hitting your bank account same day every month?

Are you prepared to give up your own funds to finance your sales and marketing activities?

Are you prepared to reallocate your personal savings to the business?
Are you prepared to give up hobbies & recreational time to spend time on the business?
Are you prepared to give up fun times with kids to work in or on the business?

Are you prepared to give up your savings to fund the business while you wait for payment?
Are you prepared to give up your lifestyle luxuries to pay staff & suppliers before yourself?
Would you like a free confidential chat to discuss your score and options?

 **Add up all your NO responses & make a note of your TOTAL
Which of the following best describes your current situation**

1. Yes. I'm all fine thanks.
2. Ah, raised some good points. Got me thinking.
3. Woa. I recognise I need to take action at some point.
4. This is all too overwhelming. I need help with this – fast.
5. I'm going to focus on my top 3 priorities from the list.

Your Financial Position

Identify what's holding you back and preventing you from becoming self-employed or starting your own business. Answer each of the questions below, then complete the exercise at the end of the section.

Do you currently have a full time job or career?
Do you currently have a part-time job or career?
Do you know the value of your knowledge, skills and experience?

Do you have a pension?
Do you have savings?
Do you have passive income streams?

Do you have prepared net worth statement and monthly budget?
Do you know the value of all your assets?
Can you sell any of your assets?

Can you release equity from any of your assets?
Can you create a rental income from any of your assets?
Do you know how much you owe and to whom?

Have you negotiated the best terms with creditors and suppliers?
Have got a new business idea or spotted a gap in the market?
Have you created a new product or service that no-one else has?

Are you getting the best rate with your utility bills?
Are you getting the best rates with your bank?
Are you getting the best rates with your credit card(s)?

Do you use shopping comparison sites?
Do you use amazon for buying goods and products?
Do you use ebay for buying products, goods and services?

Do you sell anything on ebay?

Have you signed up to any affiliate programs?

Do you sell advertising on your website?

Are you entitled to any government subsidies, benefits or handouts?

Are you entitled to any financial compensation or award?

Are you eligible for any scholarships, grants or disbursements?

Are you eligible for a pay rise?

Have you thought about getting a new or different job?

Have you considered teaching others what you know or can do?

Have you considered coaching others what you know or can do?

Have you thought about writing a book, ebook or audio program about what you know?

Have you thought of all the ways you can reduce your monthly expenditure?

Would you like a free confidential chat to discuss your score and options?

Add up all your NO responses & make a note of your TOTAL
Which of the following best describes your current situation

1. Yes. I'm all fine thanks.
2. Ah, raised some good points. Got me thinking.
3. Woa. I recognise I need to take action at some point.
4. This is all too overwhelming. I need help with this – fast.
5. I'm going to focus on my top 3 priorities from the list.

Part 2 – Start-Up

Your Disruptive Business Model

Identify what's holding you back and preventing you from becoming self-employed or starting your own business. Answer each of the questions below, then complete the exercise at the end of the section.

Have You Documented Your Mission & Vision?
Have You Documented Your Business Model?
Have You Documented Your Marketing Strategy?

Have You Defined & Documented Your Business Values?
Have You Created a Prospect & Ideal Client Profile?
Are Your Values Aligned with Your Customer's Needs?

Are Your Values Aligned with Your Customer's Values?
Do any of your competitors offer a better "deal "than you?
Are there ways you can improve your existing "proposition"?

Do you have clearly defined market segments?
Are there segments that you have NOT targeted yet?
Is your market or could it become – saturated within the next 5 years?

Do you have clearly defined delivery channels?
Are you using delivery channels not used by your competitors?
Are you using delivery channels that have or could shortly become obsolete?

Are you winning business & customers that your competitors used to have?
Are competitors winning business & customers that you used to have?
Do you have a high customer retention and low attrition rate?

Do you eliminate something for clients that your competitors can't or don't?

Do you reduce something for clients that your competitors can't or don't?

Do you create something for clients that your competitors can't or don't?

Do you raise something for clients well above the industry standard?

Do you have strategic or Channel partners that your competitors don't?

Are you too dependent on a particular channel partner?

Are your competitors dependent or heavily rely on a particular partner?

Are you generating revenue from a number of diverse sources?

Is there a danger of some your revenue sources "drying up"?

Have you identified new possible revenues streams that clients are prepared to pay for?

Are the activities you currently offer – unique, "protected", and difficult to copy?

Have you identified opportunities that competitors simply haven't?

Are your activities or resources in danger of being disrupted by competitors?

Are there systems, processes, procedures or approaches you can improve?

Have you identified other resources within your business you can better exploit?

Are there frustrations & needs of customers in the industry have not being met?

Have you given up in wanting to be "disruptive" in your marketplace?

Would you like a FREE confidential Chat to discuss your score & available options?

Add up all your NO responses & make a note of your TOTAL
Which of the following best describes your current situation

1. Yes. I'm all fine thanks.
2. Ah, raised some good points. Got me thinking.
3. Woa. I recognise I need to take action at some point.
4. This is all too overwhelming. I need help with this – fast.
5. I'm going to focus on my top 3 priorities from the list.

Your Business Plan

Identify what's holding you back and preventing you from becoming self-employed or starting your own business. Answer each of the questions below, then complete the exercise at the end of the section.

Have you completed your Business Plan?

Do you know what lenders and investors like to see in a Business Plan?

Do you know what should be included in your EXECUTIVE SUMMARY?

Have you documented the size of your market & whether it's growing or declining?

Have you documented the needs of the market and how you satisfy those needs?

Have you documented what's unique about your offering?

Have you documented why an investor should invest in your new business project?

Have you included the reasons why your business project is "unique"?

Have you documented the reasons why prospects will choose you & not competitors?

Have you documented how much capital you need and what it will be used for?

Have you documented how you have eliminated or reduced as much risk as you can?

Have you documented all your intellectual property and how you've protected it?

Have you documented all your revenue streams & product "offerings"?

Do you know what ROI and/or "terms" you want with lenders and investors?

Have you calculated and documented all the necessary start-up costs?

Have you documented all your on-going monthly costs & operational requirements?

Have you considered what will be included in the appendix?

Have you clearly identified each of the different segments of your target audience?

Have you created a 12m / 3year Cash flow, Sales, Balance sheet, P & L Projection?

Have you allowed for TAX & VAT in your forecasted figures?

Has an accountant checked over your business plan and financial data?

Have you documented and included your market research and R & D to date?

Have you documented what the opportunity actually is for investors or lenders?

Have you documented what the ROI will be for lenders or Investors?

Have you documented your routes to market and how you will market your solutions?

Have you documented your sales approach, process, pricing and "terms"?

Have you documented your goals, reporting systems & Key Performance Indicators?

Have you confirmed what the barriers to entry are for competitors?

Have you written your Mission, Vision & Value Statements?

Have you & each member of your team's CV or Bio listing relevant accomplishments?

Have you documented your EXIT strategy and when it is anticipated to be?

Have you documented your marketing & promotional activities calendar?

Have you documented your business structure and existing operations?

Have you documented your requirements with regards to premises & what's needed?

Would you like a template, fill-in-the-blanks business plan to help save time & money?

Would you like a free confidential Chat to discuss your score & your available options?

Add up all your NO responses & make a note of your TOTAL
Which of the following best describes your current situation

1. Yes. I'm all fine thanks.
2. Ah, raised some good points. Got me thinking.
3. Woa. I recognise I need to take action at some point.
4. This is all too overwhelming. I need help with this – fast.
5. I'm going to focus on my top 3 priorities from the list.

General Data Protection Regulation

Identify what's holding you back and preventing you from becoming self-employed or starting your own business. Answer each of the questions below, then complete the exercise at the end of the section.

Do you know how the General Data Protection Regulation (GDPR) will affect your business?
Do you know what the requirements of the GDPR are?
Do you have a plan for how you will become GDPR compliant?

Have you documented what personal data you hold?
Have you documented where the personal data came from?
Have you documented with whom you share personal data?

Have you reviewed your current privacy notices?
Have you a plan for changing your privacy notices?
Do you know what changes you need to make in order to comply?

Do your procedures cover all the rights that individuals have?
Do your procedures allow individuals to delete their personal data?
Do your systems help you locate and delete data?

Have you documented how you will handle subject access requests (SARs)?
Will you be able to respond to Subject Access Requests (SARs) within 30 Days?
Do you have a plan for how you will handle subject access requests (SARs)?

Have you identified the lawful basis for your processing in the GDPR?
Do you have a method to document how you process personal data?
Have you updated your privacy notice to reflect the lawful basis for processing personal data?

Have you reviewed how you seek, record and manage consent in your marketing funnel?
Do you know how to translate GDPR compliance into a practical plan to generate NEW leads?
Do you know how many leads you need to generate the revenue you want in 2018?

Have you written a marketing plan that will translate GDPR readiness into leads and sales?
Do you have a practical system in place for measuring your marketing plan's daily ROI?
Do you have a practical system for demonstrating to stakeholders/shareholders its working?

Do you have a practical GDPR Ready system for filling your funnel & pipeline in 2018?
Do you have a practical system for holding marketing staff, VAs & Agencies accountable?
Do you have a practical system in place to avoid repeating the marketing challenges of 2017?

Do you have procedures in place to detect, report & investigate a personal data breach (PDB)?
Do you have a procedure in place to report a PDB to the ICO?
Do you have a system in place to verify individuals' ages & obtain parental consent?

Is it you that's taking responsibility for data protection compliance?
Do you need to formally designate a data protection officer (DPO)?

Have you assessed where the DPO will be in your org's structure?

Does your organisation operate in more than one EU member state? Would you like a FREE confidential Chat to discuss your score & your available options?

Add up all your NO responses & make a note of your TOTAL
Which of the following best describes your current situation

1. Yes. I'm all fine thanks.
2. Ah, raised some good points. Got me thinking.
3. Woa. I recognise I need to take action at some point.
4. This is all too overwhelming. I need help with this – fast.
5. I'm going to focus on my top 3 priorities from the list.

Innovation

Identify what's holding you back and preventing you from becoming self-employed or starting your own business. Answer each of the questions below, then complete the exercise at the end of the section.

Do you have an innovation policy?

Do you have an innovation strategy document or "Master Plan"?

Do you have staff with the correct innovative skills, talent, knowledge & experience?

Do you have processes, procedures & methods in place to capture/create ideas?

Do you invest in training in areas like innovation, problem solving, marketing?

Do you recruit staff from other countries?

Do you perform research and development (R&D) within your organisation?

Do you have external organisations perform research & development on your behalf?

Do you know what the latest Trends, Needs & Frustrations are in your industry?

Do you purchase or licence patents, copyrighted materials or other knowledge?

Do you invest in training & support in innovative areas?

Have you acquired new plant, machinery, equipment or software?

Is your USP - the development of new unique products, services & processes?

Is your USP - the development of new business models & ways to market?

41

Is your USP - the reduction of costs in existing products and services?

Within your organisational structure, is it free from duplication of tasks or effort?
Are your business processes free from bottlenecks or delays in execution?
Are your business processes automated and as efficient as possible?

Have you designed (or purchased) new graphics, packaging, processes, or products?
Have you applied for NEW patents, copyright, business names or trademarks?
Have you protected your existing intellectual property?

Do you outsource tasks (or work) to companies in other countries?
Do you invest in other companies in other countries?
Do you market test your products in other countries?

Do you supply customers only within a local/regional or national geographical area?
Do you supply customers within the EU and countries like Norway or Switzerland?
Do you supply customers globally (outside of the EU)?

Have you created any collaborations/strategic relationships with other companies?
Have you created any partnerships/collaborations with research institutes?
Have you created any strategic relationships/partnerships with educational institutes?

Are you aware of the latest tax developments in the area of innovation or R&D?
Are you aware of the latest public financial support in the area of

innovation or R&D?

Have you identified an increased demand in energy efficient or sustainable products?

Have you identified an emergence of new technologies that could be exploited?

Have you identified NEW export opportunities in any newly emerging countries?

Would you like a free confidential Chat to discuss your score & your available options?

 Add up all your NO responses & make a note of your TOTAL
Which of the following best describes your current situation

1. Yes. I'm all fine thanks.
2. Ah, raised some good points. Got me thinking.
3. Woa. I recognise I need to take action at some point.
4. This is all too overwhelming. I need help with this – fast.
5. I'm going to focus on my top 3 priorities from the list.

Market Research

Identify what's holding you back and preventing you from growing your existing business. Answer each of the questions below, then complete the exercise at the end of the section.

Do you know if your target market has "changed"?

Do you know if your marketplace is growing, declining or stagnating?

Do you have a clear definition of what the "Opportunity" is and why have the solution?

Do you know of any businesses in the market you could acquire for a faster route to market?

Do you know of any products in the market you could acquire the rights to?

Do you know what's new, what's hot, what the "buzz" is & what the top sellers are?

Do you know who your top 10 local, national & online competitors are?

Do you know who your top 10 local national & online influencers are?

Do you know who the leading thought leaders, experts & "authorities" are in your industry?

Do you know what margin % you will generate from each product, service or solution?

Do you know how much you should be charging for your time on a day rate or hourly rate?

Do you know what value your competitors offer for the prices they charge?

Do you know what all your revenue streams will be for what you plan to sell?

Do you know how many leads you need to achieve your revenue objectives?

Do you have a formal referral strategy in place to refer you sales opportunities?

Do you know what the top 10 customer needs are, in the industry?
Do you know what the top 10 things customers WANT in the industry?
Do you know what the top 10 customer frustrations are, in the industry?

Do you know what questions potential clients are already asking when looking for a solution?
Do you know what the demand is for your products and services you plan to offer?
Do you know what keywords prospects are typing in, to find your competitors online?

Do you know who your competitors are targeting and why?
Do you know which channels your competitors are using to promote their services?
Do you know which engagement tactics your competitors are using?

Do you WHY prospective customers do business with your competitors instead of you?
Do you how your competitors are generating leads and building their list?
Do you know what price and "value" your competitors are offering?

Do you have a website in place to service and educate your target market?
Do you have a marketing funnel in place to pull people to you and create sales opportunities?
Do you have a clearly defined sales process in place to convert opportunities into revenue?
Have you had adequate training in marketing to be able to generate leads daily?

Have you had adequate sales training to be able to close sales daily?

Do you have the technical solutions in place to automate your prospecting & lead generation?

Do you know which tools and resources to use to validate the size of your opportunity?

Do you have a written plan to document the opportunity & how you will service the demand?

Would you like a FREE confidential Chat to discuss your score & available options?

 Add up all your NO responses & make a note of your TOTAL
Which of the following best describes your current situation

1. Yes. I'm all fine thanks.
2. Ah, raised some good points. Got me thinking.
3. Woa. I recognise I need to take action at some point.
4. This is all too overwhelming. I need help with this – fast.
5. I'm going to focus on my top 3 priorities from the list.

Investing & Funding

Identify what's holding you back and preventing you from becoming self-employed or starting your own business. Answer each of the questions below, then complete the exercise at the end of the section.

Have you documented your model, vision and strategy?
Have you got an EXIT Strategy, clearly documented?
Have you prepared cash flow, Profit & Loss, Break-Even & Sales Projections?

Do you have private investors you can approach for funding?
Do you have any business angels you can approach for funding?
Do you know any venture capitalists (VCs) you can approach for funding?

Do you know the size & value of your market?
Do you know the current trends in your market?
Do you know why you're better than your competitors & who they are?

Do you know exactly who your potential customers are?
Do you know what the expected life time value of a customer will be?
Do you know what problems (and the impact/cost of them) that you solve for customers?

Do you know how much funding you require, and when it will be repaid?
Do you know exactly what the money is needed for?
Do you know exactly what all the revenue streams are for your business model?
Have you defined ALL your routes to market?
Have you defined each step in your sales process?

Have you got a clearly defined unique selling point or unique business advantage?

Have you assembled your management team and identified their skill gaps?

Do you know your typical cost per lead, cost per sale & profit margin per sale?

Have you established a fair market valuation for your business now?

Have you protected your business name, idea and all intellectual property?

Have you got the appropriate reporting systems & financial systems in place?

Have you got clearly defined objectives, milestones & a plan of action to achieve them?

Do you have a proof of concept, prototype or "working model"?

Do you have existing customers, signed agreements or signed letters of intent?

Have you secured the required strategic, channel or technology partners?

Do you how much equity you want to give away, need to give away or have to give away?

Do you know what your investors want in return for giving you the investment you need?

Do you know when investors want to exit & the impact that will have on the business?

Do you know what your stage of development is & how much you've spent to date?

Do you know how long your "window of opportunity" will exist for?

Do you know what the implications are if you do not get the

finance/investment you need?

Would you like to be introduced to personal investors who might be interested?

Have you completed your business plan & got different versions for different audiences?

Would you like a FREE chat to discuss your score, and available /potential options?

Add up all your NO responses & make a note of your TOTAL
Which of the following best describes your current situation

1. Yes. I'm all fine thanks.
2. Ah, raised some good points. Got me thinking.
3. Woa. I recognise I need to take action at some point.
4. This is all too overwhelming. I need help with this – fast.
5. I'm going to focus on my top 3 priorities from the list.

Protecting Your Idea & Business

Identify what's holding you back and preventing you from becoming self-employed or starting your own business.   Answer each of the questions below, then complete the exercise at the end of the section.

Have you protected your idea?
Have you come up with a name for your idea or business?
Have you protected your name?

Have you documented and protected your tangible assets?
Have you documented and protected your intangible assets"?
Have you protected yourself, your business against IPR theft from staff?

Have you documented and protected your systems, processes & procedures?
Have you documented and protected your designs, artwork, logo, images, photos etc?
Have you documented and protected your software?

Have you documented and protected your sales and marketing information?
Have you documented and protected your manufacturing and operational information?
Have you documented and protected your recipes, ingredients or formulations?

Have you documented and protected your Research & Development work?
Have you documented and protected any collaborative work produced with 3rd parties?
Have you documented and protected all financial information and systems?

Have you documented and protected any video, music or audio IPR?

Have you documented and protected all your "trade secrets"?
Have you applied for and secured any trademark registrations?

Have you applied for and secured any patent registrations?
Have you copyrighted all works that you have produced or created?

Have you documented and protected all intellectual property shared with staff?

Have you documented and protected all intellectual property shared with partners?
Have you documented and protected all intellectual property shared with suppliers?
Have you documented and protected all intellectual property shared with customers?

Have you documented and protected all "published" works such as articles, books etc.?
Have you documented and protected all digital assets such as PDFs, PPTX, and DOCX etc.?
Have you identified and documented the owners of the intellectual property you use?

Have you taken steps to mitigate or reduce risk or confusion over any IPR you use?
Have you recently made an amendments to existing trademark or patent applications?
Have you documented all contracted and agreements that you share with contractors?

Do you plan to license, share or rent out any of your intellectual property or assets?

Have you recently bought or sold a tangible or intangible asset?
Do you know if you're losing revenue by not monetising your intellectual capital?

Have you had any of your intellectual property professionally valued?
Would you like to secure, and protect your intellectual property?
Would you like a FREE Chat to discuss your score and available options?

Add up all your NO responses & make a note of your TOTAL
Which of the following best describes your current situation

1. Yes. I'm all fine thanks.
2. Ah, raised some good points. Got me thinking.
3. Woa. I recognise I need to take action at some point.
4. This is all too overwhelming. I need help with this – fast.
5. I'm going to focus on my top 3 priorities from the list.

Branding

Identify what's holding you back and preventing you from becoming self-employed or starting your own business. Answer each of the questions below, then complete the exercise at the end of the section.

Have you protected your idea?
Have you come up with a name for your idea or business?
Have you protected your name?

Have you documented and protected your tangible assets?
Have you documented and protected your intangible assets"?
Have you protected yourself, your business against IPR theft from staff?

Have you documented and protected your systems, processes & procedures?
Have you documented and protected your designs, artwork, logo, images, photos etc?
Have you documented and protected your software?

Have you documented and protected your sales and marketing information?
Have you documented and protected your manufacturing and operational information?
Have you documented and protected your recipes, ingredients or formulations?

Have you documented and protected your Research & Development work?
Have you documented and protected any collaborative work produced with 3rd parties?
Have you documented and protected all financial information and systems?

Have you documented and protected any video, music or audio IPR?

Have you documented and protected all your "trade secrets"?
Have you applied for and secured any trademark registrations?

Have you applied for and secured any patent registrations?
Have you copyrighted all works that you have produced or created?

Have you documented and protected all intellectual property shared with staff?

Have you documented and protected all intellectual property shared with partners?
Have you documented and protected all intellectual property shared with suppliers?
Have you documented and protected all intellectual property shared with customers?

Have you documented and protected all "published" works such as articles, books etc.?
Have you documented and protected all digital assets such as PDFs, PPTX, and DOCX etc?
Have you identified and documented the owners of the intellectual property you use?

Have you taken steps to mitigate or reduce risk or confusion over any IPR you use?
Have you recently made an amendments to existing trademark or patent applications?
Have you documented all contracted and agreements that you share with contractors?

Do you plan to license, share or rent out any of your intellectual property or assets?

Have you recently bought or sold a tangible or intangible asset?
Do you know if you're losing revenue by not monetising your intellectual capital?

Have you had any of your intellectual property professionally valued?
Would you like to secure, and protect your intellectual property?
Would you like a FREE Chat to discuss your score and available options?

 Add up all your NO responses & make a note of your TOTAL
Which of the following best describes your current situation

1. Yes. I'm all fine thanks.
2. Ah, raised some good points. Got me thinking.
3. Woa. I recognise I need to take action at some point.
4. This is all too overwhelming. I need help with this – fast.
5. I'm going to focus on my top 3 priorities from the list.

Human Resources

Identify what's holding you back and preventing you from becoming self-employed or starting your own business. Answer each of the questions below, then complete the exercise at the end of the section.

Will you be employing staff?
Will you be hiring sub-contractors?
Will you be hiring casual or part-time labour?

Do you have an organisation chart?
Do you know what "positions" and roles you need filled?
Do you know what tasks you would like completed & objectives you'd like to achieve?

Have you determined how much they will be compensated and how?
Have you determined what skills and talents they need to perform the task?
Have you determined what knowledge and qualifications they need to perform the task?

Have you determined what experience they need to perform the task?
Have you written a job description, or "brief"?
Have you created the necessary contracts or agreements?

Have you determined who they will be answerable to or reporting to?
Have you implemented a payroll solution?
Have you implemented a management reporting system?

Have you created the necessary policies and procedures?
Have you determined how and how often staff (or contractors) will appraised?
Have you identified what training staff and contractors will require?

Have you identified how you will keep current with employment legislation?

Will you offer any bonuses, incentives or share options to your staff?

Have you defined the roles, responsibilities & resources your staff will have or need?

Have you budgeted for the staff you will hire?

Will you qualify for any government financial "assistance" with hiring staff?

Do you have a pension scheme in place?

Do you need vehicles for your staff?

Do you need mobile phones, laptops or other specific equipment?

Do you have a system in place for addressing/dealing with staff expenses?

Will you require a dress code?

Have you created an operations handbook?

Do you have the appropriate insurances in place if you are hiring/employing staff?

Will you provide private health insurance or dental insurance?

Do you need a canteen or changing room facilities?

Do you need additional car parking?

Do you need larger premises to accommodate your growing team of staff?

Do you really need to hire staff or can you sub-contract professional help as and when?

Would you like a free confidential Chat to discuss your score & your available options?

Add up all your NO responses & make a note of your TOTAL
Which of the following best describes your current situation

1. Yes. I'm all fine thanks.
2. Ah, raised some good points. Got me thinking.
3. Woa. I recognise I need to take action at some point.
4. This is all too overwhelming. I need help with this – fast.
5. I'm going to focus on my top 3 priorities from the list.

Legal Considerations

Identify what's holding you back and preventing you from becoming self-employed or starting your own business. Answer each of the questions below, then complete the exercise at the end of the section.

Do you know what type of Business Structure/Entity you will have?
Have you registered for VAT, NI and Taxation purposes?
Have you registered and protected your business name and other relevant assets?

Does your stationery meet all the necessary legal requirements?
Does your website meet all the necessary legal requirements?
Does your emails meet all the necessary legal requirements?

Have you registered with the Information Commissioner's Office?
Have you registered for and obtained all necessary permits and licences?
Do you know what legal agreements you will require for your business?

Have you prepared all the legal agreements you will require?
Have you appointed all the required advisers that your business needs?
Do you currently comply with and follow all the relevant environmental requirements?

Have you prepared standard terms and conditions for doing business with you?
Have you read, confirmed and accepted your supplier's terms and conditions?
Have you got all the necessary insurance you require to protect you & your assets?
Have you got adequate protection for minimising and eliminating

personal risk?

Do your premises meet all the necessary legal requirements?

Have you registered all software in the business name?

Have your protected yourself in order to meet all health & safety requirements?

Have you protected yourself if you are going to be selling or BUYING online?

Has an accountant checked over your business plan & projected legal costs?

Do you have any FREE legal advice with any of your current insurance policies?

Have you protected yourself against "late payments"?

Have you taken the steps to protect your idea & prevent others from copying it?

Do you have adequate legal protection for when dealing with investors & lenders?

Do you have adequate legal protection in the event that you are negligent?

Do you have adequate legal protection in the event that you fall ill?

Do you have adequate legal protection in the event of your staff being negligent?

Do you have adequate legal protection in the event of your suppliers being negligent?

Do you have adequate legal protection if clients or suppliers take legal action?

Do you have adequate legal protection for all your assets and your property?

Have you got all the necessary legal agreements in place that you will need?

Have you got all the necessary legal licenses or permissions that you need?

Do you have a solicitor and are they helping you protect your business?

Do you know have a source of free legal advice?

Would you like a free confidential Chat to discuss your score & your available options?

 Add up all your NO responses & make a note of your TOTAL
Which of the following best describes your current situation

1. Yes. I'm all fine thanks.
2. Ah, raised some good points. Got me thinking.
3. Woa. I recognise I need to take action at some point.
4. This is all too overwhelming. I need help with this – fast.
5. I'm going to focus on my top 3 priorities from the list.

Technology

Identify what's holding you back and preventing you from becoming self-employed or starting your own business. Answer each of the questions below, then complete the exercise at the end of the section.

Do you know what hardware you require?
Do you know what software you require?
Do you know what pinkware (people) you require?

Do you know what netware you require?
Have you ensured you are using business and not personal versions of software?
Do you know what internet connection you need?

Have you registered a domain name?
Have you got an email address and email account set up?
Have you got an autoresponder or CRM system set up?

Do you have a solution for scanning, copying and printing documents?
Do you have a technology solution to assist you in managing your projects for clients?
Do you have a technology solution to assist you in the collaboration with others?

Are you registered with the Information Commissioner's Office?
Do you have a written privacy and social media policy?
Do you have a written terms of service for your website?

Do you have a website?
Do you have a smart phone?
Does your website render correctly for mobile devices?

Do you perform a daily, weekly or monthly backup schedule?

Is your data stored offsite or in the "cloud"?

Is your network configured correctly and all users given appropriate permissions?

Do you synchronise your laptop/pc with your smartphone to minimise data loss?

Do you accept, make or manage your accounting data via your phone or internet?

Have you got a unified communications and mobile strategy?

Have you protected your data and website from viruses, trojans and malware?

Have you appointed a web designer, copywriter and marketer for your website?

Have you created a content strategy & all the necessary digital assets that you require?

Have you vetted, approved and appointed your I.T. & Internet Solution Supplier?

Do you have 24/7 365 Support?

Have you created a maintenance and service schedule for your equipment?

Have you got a firewall set up on your network?

Do you have CCTV or security systems set up for your premises?

Have you identified all the software and training you and your staff may require?

Have you identified the key business processes that technology will help you improve?

Have you identified the objectives you want to achieve with the technology in your business?

Would you like a free confidential Chat to discuss your score & your available options?

Add up all your NO responses & make a note of your TOTAL
Which of the following best describes your current situation

1. Yes. I'm all fine thanks.
2. Ah, raised some good points. Got me thinking.
3. Woa. I recognise I need to take action at some point.
4. This is all too overwhelming. I need help with this – fast.
5. I'm going to focus on my top 3 priorities from the list.

Routes to Market

Identify what's holding you back and preventing you from becoming self-employed or starting your own business. Answer each of the questions below, then complete the exercise at the end of the section.

Do you currently use direct mail to reach your target audience?
Do you currently use channel partners or JV partners?
Do you currently use a sales team, distributors or agents?

Do you currently use Live video streaming to reach your audience or target market?
Do you currently use webinars or video marketing?
Do you currently use workshops?

Do you currently use telemarketing or telecanvassing?
Do you currently use teleconferences?
Do you currently use party plan or network marketing?

Do you know which directories you're listed on?
Do you currently use social bookmarking tools to help site visitors promote you?
Do you currently create infographics?

Do you currently use social networking?
Do you currently use business networking?
Do you currently use document or image sharing sites?

Do you currently use importers/exporters?
Do you currently use wholesalers & retailers?
Do you currently use affiliates or drop shippers?

Do you currently have any books, e-books or courses published?

Do you currently use leaflet distribution?
Do you currently have a referral marketing system?

Do you currently have any audio books published?
Do you currently have an podcasts published?
Do you currently use itunes to reach your target market?

Do you currently have an SEO or PPC (Pay per click) Strategy?
Do you currently position yourself as a keynote speaker or guest speaker?
Do you currently position yourself as a blogger, vlogger or guest blogger?

Do you use classified or paid advertising online?
Do you use classified or display advertising offline?
Do you currently share APPS, widgets or extensions in google play store?
Do you currently write emails, articles or send a regular e-zine to reach your audience?
Do you attend, visit, sponsor or speak at exhibitions, tradeshows or industry events?
Do you use Public Relations tactics online and offline?

Do you control or process any personal identifiable information as part of your marketing?
Do you acquire and document consent at each stage of your marketing process?
Would you like a free confidential Chat to discuss your score and available options?

Add up all your NO responses & make a note of your TOTAL
Which of the following best describes your current situation

1. Yes. I'm all fine thanks.
2. Ah, raised some good points. Got me thinking.
3. Woa. I recognise I need to take action at some point.
4. This is all too overwhelming. I need help with this – fast.
5. I'm going to focus on my top 3 priorities from the list.

Start-up Costs

Identify what's holding you back and preventing you from becoming self-employed or starting your own business. Answer each of the questions below, then complete the exercise at the end of the section.

Do you know your net worth?
Do you know how much you owe and to whom?
Do you know what your monthly incomings and outgoings currently are?

Do you know what start-up costs you need to become self-employed or start your business?
Do you know what your monthly overheads will be?
Do you know how much investment or borrowings you need & specifically why you need it?

Do you know how much revenue you need/want for the next 12 months?
Do you know how many sales you need/want for the next 12 months?
Do you know how many leads you need/want for the next 12 months?

Do you know how many referrals you need/want for the next 12 months?
Do you know what your profit margin is for what you'll be offering?
Do you know how much of a salary/drawings you (and others) will need/want?

Have you calculated a monthly budget that you need to operate within for 12 months?
Have you researched and compared supplier terms?
Have you identified all your direct and indirect costs?

Have you taken the necessary VAT or TAX advice and preparations?

Do you know what payroll software or solutions you will use?

Do you know what book keeping or accounting system you will use?

Have you created a 3 year Cash flow, Sales, Balance sheet, B/E or P & L Projection?

Do you know what ROI you can offer investors or repayments to lenders?

Has an accountant checked over your business plan and financial data?

Do you know how much you can afford to pay for a sale and for a lead?

Have you investigated any "soft loans" or government loans?

Have you calculated what your pricing or daily/hourly fees should be?

Do you have a pension, benefits or share option scheme in place for yourself or staff?

Will you be accepting credit card payments online, offline or both?

Have you vetted and compared potential suppliers, and confirmed best VALUE?

Does your business model contain passive revenue streams?

Do you know the impact discounting or price increases will have on your cash flow?

Do you know what information an investor or lender wants or needs?

Do you know what profit margins you'll have with each of the solutions you'll offer?

Have you set your own credit terms and terms of service?

Do you know what impact late payers will have on your business model?

Is your accountant helping you prepare the words of your business plan & financials?

Have you checked out at least 10 different sources of funding & whether you actually need it?

Would you like a free confidential Chat to discuss your score & your available options?

Add up all your NO responses & make a note of your TOTAL
Which of the following best describes your current situation

1. Yes. I'm all fine thanks.
2. Ah, raised some good points. Got me thinking.
3. Woa. I recognise I need to take action at some point.
4. This is all too overwhelming. I need help with this – fast.
5. I'm going to focus on my top 3 priorities from the list.

Part 3 – Survival

Time Management

Identify what's holding you back and preventing you from becoming self-employed or starting your own business. Answer each of the questions below, then complete the exercise at the end of the section.

Do you know how many hours you spend a week - online?
Do you know how many hours you spend a week – writing letters, proposals & emails?
Do you know how many hours you spend a week – on the phone?

Do you know how many hours you spend a week – on appointments?
Do you know how many hours you spend a week - at networking events?
Do you know your cost or rate per hour?

Do you know how much of your time per week is spent - Researching?
Do you know how much of your time per week is spent - Planning?
Do you know how much of your time per week is spent - Prospecting?

Do you know how much of your time per week is spent - Selling?
Do you know how much of your time per week is spent – Servicing existing clients?
Do you know how much of your time per week is spent - Watching TV?

Do you know how much of your time per week is spent – Supporting/Helping Clients?
Do you know how much of your time per week is spent – On Administrative tasks?
Do you know how much of your time per week is spent – Travelling?
Do you know how much of your time per week is spent – Domestic chores?

Do you know how much of your time per week is spent – On developing personal skills?

Do you know how much of your time per week is spent – Caring for others?

Do you set quarterly monthly, weekly and daily goals and objectives?

Do you prioritise your day with a "TO DO" list?

Do you review your end of day and update your goals & "TO DO" list?

Do you delegate, sub-contract & set deadlines for your prospecting tasks?

Do you delegate, sub-contract & set deadlines for your follow-up tasks?

Do you delegate, sub-contract & set deadlines for your sales support tasks?

Do you delegate, sub-contract & set deadlines for your admin tasks?

Do you delegate, sub-contract & set deadlines for your customer service tasks?

Do you tackle and do the "worst things, first" each day?

Do you set time limits for each meeting agenda item?

Do you set distance limits for travelling to an appointment?

Do you set time limits for being out of the office to attend appointments?

Do you set aside time per week to work on your "sales strategy"?

Do you set aside time per week in your diary for "me time" and "hobbies"?

Do you know what your "chargeable time/non chargeable time"ratio is?

Do you ensure you focus on outcomes and not activities?

Do you stay focussed by prioritising on the tasks you MUST,

SHOULD & COULD do?

Would you like a free confidential Chat to discuss your score and options?

Add up all your NO responses & make a note of your TOTAL
Which of the following best describes your current situation

1. Yes. I'm all fine thanks.
2. Ah, raised some good points. Got me thinking.
3. Woa. I recognise I need to take action at some point.
4. This is all too overwhelming. I need help with this – fast.
5. I'm going to focus on my top 3 priorities from the list.

Revisiting Your Sales Message

Identify what's holding you back and preventing you from growing your existing business. Answer each of the questions below, then complete the exercise at the end of the section.

Do you have a written marketing communications strategy document?
Do you have a portfolio of offline marketing collateral?
Do you write all your own sales & marketing "copy"?

Do you have a portfolio of "lead magnets", digital assets or "value BONUSes" ?
Do you host your own webinars?
Do you produce your own videos?

Do you currently have a squeeze page or landing page on your website?
Do you currently have a video sales page on your website?
Do you currently have a blog page on your website?

Do you have a prepared list of product/service facts, features and benefits?
Do you have a prepared list of customer needs, pains or frustrations?
Do you have a prepared list of answers for objections or FAQs?

Have you written/created a Brand "promise"?
Have you created an elevator pitch, 30 second commercial or telemarketing script?
Have you created a speaker's kit?

Do you guest blog on other people's sites?
Are you a panellist or guest on other people's webinars or live events?
Have you prepared a portfolio of workshop scripts?

Do you have a private members area or community area on your site?

Do you have a collection of CTAs (calls to action)?

Do you upsell website visitors and customers with OTOs (one time offers)?

Do you have a collection of headlines to test and use for blogs, ads, articles etc.?

Do you have a collection of classified ads to test and use for distributing online & offline?

Do you have a collection of images/photos to test and use for sharing online?

Do you have a portfolio of electronic & hard copy marketing collateral / promotional material?

Do you publish a regular monthly newsletter?

Do you have an autoresponder sequence set up on your website?

Do you have a collection of status updates, micro blogs or tweets that you test & use?

Do you have a Video Sales Letter on your website?

Do you have a Webinar page / platform connected to your website?

Have you created a webinar presentation?

Have you created a webinar script & framework?

Have you created multiple webinar closes and trial closes?

Have you created a compelling sales message on the sales page of your website?

Do you have a written strategy & blue print to address all your copywriting requirements?

Would you like a FREE confidential Chat to discuss your score & available options?

Add up all your NO responses & make a note of your TOTAL

Which of the following best describes your current situation

1. Yes. I'm all fine thanks.
2. **Ah, raised some good points. Got me thinking.**
3. **Woa. I recognise I need to take action at some point.**
4. **This is all too overwhelming. I need help with this – fast.**
5. **I'm going to focus on my top 3 priorities from the list.**

Marketing & Sales Prospecting

Identify what's holding you back and preventing you from growing your existing business.   Answer each of the questions below, then complete the exercise at the end of the section.

Do you have a completed prospect profile for who you're targeting?
Do you know where your potential customers congregate online?
Have defined how many steps you have in your current sales process?

Do you segment your market to better target prospective clients?
Do you segment your market by geography?
Do you segment by individual product, service or revenue stream?

Do you know how many leads you need to achieve the revenue you want?
Do you know how much website traffic you need to achieve the revenue you want?
Do you know how many referrals you need to achieve the revenue you want?

Have you created a lead magnet, digital asset or free item of value?
Have you created a list of pains, needs & frustrations of your prospective customers?
Have you created an advocate profile?

Do you know your current cost per lead?
Do you know your current cost per sales?
Do you know the life time value of a client?

Do you know who can refer you clients?
Do you know how to be kept up-to-date what prospective clients are doing online?
Do you know which channels & routes to market your competitors are

using online?

Do you currently have an automated prospecting system to pull people into your funnel?
Do you currently have an automated sales process for closing sales & generating revenue?
Do you currently have an automated follow-up system to maximise sales conversions?

Do you know what prospective clients will pay a premium for?
Do you know what prospective clients DO NOT want?
Do you know what questions prospective clients are likely to ask?

Do you know why prospective clients will want to do business with you?
Do you know why prospective clients will NOT want to do business with you?
Do you know why prospective clients will want to do business with your competitors?

Do you know how much you can afford to spend to acquire a lead?
Do you know how much you can afford to spend to acquire an appointment?
Do you know how much you can afford to spend to acquire a sale?

Do you have a prepared elevator pitch/"30 Second Commercial" for use on the phone?
Do you have a prospecting email that is effective and proven to create new relationships?
Do you have lots of social proof and digital assets to prove you excel at what you offer?

Have you positioned yourself as an author/thought leader, & speaker to generate leads?
Are you serious in wanting to better target people who might need or

want your solutions?
Would you like a FREE confidential chat to discuss your score & available options?

Add up all your NO responses & make a note of your TOTAL
Which of the following best describes your current situation

1. Yes. I'm all fine thanks.
2. Ah, raised some good points. Got me thinking.
3. Woa. I recognise I need to take action at some point.
4. This is all too overwhelming. I need help with this – fast.
5. I'm going to focus on my top 3 priorities from the list.

Sales & Selling

Identify what's holding you back and preventing you from growing your existing business. Answer each of the questions below, then complete the exercise at the end of the section.

Do you have a written sales plan document?
Do you have a sales team?
Do you (and your team) have and follow a specific selling "system"?

Do you prepare and present a sales presentation of features & benefits for appointments?
Do you quantify the financial impact of prospective client's problems, needs and pain?
Do you leave the "money" and asking for the order until the end of your appointment?

Are you generating enough new prospects who are interested in your services?
Are you closing enough prospects, and converting enough sales/revenue?
Are you always getting sales without having to discount or reduce your asking price?

Are you generating enough new referrals every month?
Are you generating enough new customers/clients every month?
Are you generating enough new leads, connections and appointment every month?

Do you use webinar marketing or Live video streaming events to sell to your audience?
Do you find yourself giving lots of information at meetings but getting little in return?
Do you win business without having to give a written sales proposal?

Do you have an automated prospecting system?

Do you send out a newsletter or e-zine on a regular basis?

Do you receive daily reporting updates of how many new relationships you've created?

Do you have an automated follow up system?

Do you know how many steps you have in your sales process?

Do you have other value added items you can use to increase or reduce the price?

Do you know how many sales you need to give you the revenue you want?

Do you know how many leads you need to give you the revenue you want?

Do you have a clear definition of what a lead is and what it means to you?

Are you ahead of your projected figures for where you should be in your plan?

Do you produce a monthly P & L for your business?

Does your sales collateral address the doubts, concerns, needs & frustrations of prospects?

Do you always find yourself speaking to the decision maker at appointments?

Are prospects always quick to return your calls when you follow them up afterwards?

Do you have an active and effective referral generation programme?

Do you have a clearly defined sales message for each stage of your sales process?

Do you currently use webinars or workshops as part of your sales process?

Do you currently use video marketing or video streaming as part of your sales process?

Do you send a sales proposal after every sales appointment?
Does every sales proposal get accepted?
Would you like a free confidential Chat to discuss your score & your available options?

Add up all your NO responses & make a note of your TOTAL
Which of the following best describes your current situation

1. Yes. I'm all fine thanks.
2. Ah, raised some good points. Got me thinking.
3. Woa. I recognise I need to take action at some point.
4. This is all too overwhelming. I need help with this – fast.
5. I'm going to focus on my top 3 priorities from the list.

Marketing Systems

Identify what's holding you back and preventing you from growing your existing business. Answer each of the questions below, then complete the exercise at the end of the section.

Do you have a clearly defined sales and your marketing process and funnel?

Is your online marketing funnel and sales process integrated into your website?

Does your website comply with GDPR requirements?

Do you have a clearly defined sales message for each step in your marketing funnel?

Do you have a technical solution in place for each step of your marketing funnel?

Do you have an automated process for following up, closing and up-selling prospects?

Have you created a FREE item of value to PULL people into your marketing funnel?

Have you created web graphic for your digital asset or FREE item of value?

Have you created a system for sales prospecting and generating leads online?

Have you created all the offline marketing collateral you need?

Have you created all the online marketing collateral you need?

Have you created a members area or community area for your website?

Have you created multiple revenue streams?

Have you created multiple passive revenue streams?

Have you created multiple squeeze/landing pages for your website?

Do you currently use video in your marketing funnel or sales process?
Do you currently use video sales letters on your website?
Do you currently use webinars in your marketing funnel or sales process?

Do you have a current back linking strategy?
Do you have a current content strategy and content development calendar?
Do you have a current posting strategy and daily schedule?

Do you automate any aspect of your lead generation or prospecting?
Do you automate any aspect of your video production or video marketing?
Do you automate any aspect of your content posting?

Do you have an appointment booking system integrated into your website?
Do you have a webinar registration system integrated into your website?
Do you sell access to your webinar content?

Have you created a pop-up light box for capturing leads into your funnel?
Have you created a slide-in box for capturing leads into your funnel?
Have you created a ribbon box for capturing leads into your funnel?

Do you have an upsell strategy in place for increasing the life time value of your customers?
Do you use live video streaming as part of your sales and marketing?
Do you have daily/real-time reporting how many people you have in your network or funnel?

Would you like to automate your prospecting and selling online?

Would you like to have all the sales copy & messages written for each stage of the process?

Would you like a FREE confidential Chat to discuss your score & your available options?

Add up all your NO responses & make a note of your TOTAL
Which of the following best describes your current situation

1. Yes. I'm all fine thanks.
2. Ah, raised some good points. Got me thinking.
3. Woa. I recognise I need to take action at some point.
4. This is all too overwhelming. I need help with this – fast.
5. I'm going to focus on my top 3 priorities from the list.

Cash flow

Identify what's holding you back and preventing you from becoming self-employed or starting your own business. Answer each of the questions below, then complete the exercise at the end of the section.

Do you have a written credit policy?
Do you have a written terms of business?
Do you have a written credit application form?

Do you perform credit checks on new client accounts?
Do you have credit limits on new client accounts?
Have your staff had training in credit assessment, collection or legal procedures?

Do you produce an aged debtor report on a monthly basis?
Are your payment terms reviewed annually?
Do your sales meetings include a review of overdue accounts?

Do you have a designated credit control department?
Do you have a designated credit control member of staff?
Do you outsource your credit control to an external agency?

Do you know how much debt and outstanding payments you have?
Do you know what the average debt per client/customer is?
Do you have any debts outstanding over 90 days?

Do you know what your competitor's payment terms are?
Do you know what the industry average or norm is?
Do your customers regularly exceed your payment terms?

Do you compete by offering longer credit terms than your competitors?

Does your product, service or solution cost more than your competitors?

Do you know what giving credit to customers actually costs your company per year?

Do you know what it costs you to administer your invoices & statements?

Do you know what it costs you to send collection letters & make collection calls?

Do you know what it costs you in accountancy fees per annum?

Do you know your DSO (Days Sales Outstanding) for last month?

Is that acceptable?

Could the bad debt of the last 12 months have been avoided with good credit control?

Do you produce a monthly report of how much cash was collected against target?

Do you produce a Brought Forward, Raised, Resolved, Carried Forward monthly report?

Do you produce a monthly report of total bad debt & next month's cash & DSO target?

Do you produce a monthly report of number & value of accounts with solicitors?

Do you produce a monthly report of all sales accounts with debt collection agency?

Do you know the legal entity/status of each of your customers?

Do you invoice promptly?

Do you request full or part payment up front?

Would you like a free confidential chat to discuss the above & your available options?

Add up all your NO responses & make a note of your TOTAL
Which of the following best describes your current situation

1. Yes. I'm all fine thanks.
2. Ah, raised some good points. Got me thinking.
3. Woa. I recognise I need to take action at some point.
4. This is all too overwhelming. I need help with this – fast.
5. I'm going to focus on my top 3 priorities from the list.

CRM

Identify what's holding you back and preventing you from growing your existing business. Answer each of the questions below, then complete the exercise at the end of the section.

Are your customer segments clearly defined?
Have you created an ideal customer profile?
Do you know what data elements you need to store about your clients?

Have you set your CRM goals and objectives?
Can each goal be tracked and measured?
Do you have a CRM solution in place?

Does your current CRM system integrate with your social networks?
Is your CRM solution accessed just by your sales team?
Is your CRM system integrated into your sales order processing/invoicing system?

Do you know how many steps you have in your sales process?
Is each step in your process clearly defined?
Do you know how many people are at each step in the process at any one time?

Do you know the source(s) of where your leads are coming from?
Are you satisfied with the level of business coming from each source?
Are you clear on what criteria must be satisfied before sending out a proposal?

Do you have an automated lead generation/prospect list building tool?
Do you have a free offer that helps to qualify prospects in advance of meeting them?

Do you always track your prospecting and sales activities on a daily basis?

Do you always follow up a lead?

Do you follow up the non-converting leads?

Do you disqualify your non converting leads?

Do you know how many sales you need to give you the revenue you want?

Do you know how many leads you need to give you the revenue you want?

Do you know how many points of contact it takes to convert a lead into sale?

Do you use a CRM system for your event management?

Do you use a CRM system for your email marketing?

Do you use a CRM system for your telemarketing?

Do you get a lot of Requests for Information/Proposals (RFI/RFP)?

Do you have a defined process for dealing with such requests?

Are you happy with the conversion to sale from such requests?

Do you have a system in place for managing customer /technical support?

Are your smart phone(s), tablet(s) & Desk top machine(s) all synched & up to date?

Do you have an automated follow up system to actively pursue sales opportunities?

Do you know the value of your client "database" at the moment?

Do you know the value of your leads and prospect database at the moment?

Would you like a FREE confidential Chat to discuss your score & your available options?

Add up all your NO responses & make a note of your TOTAL
Which of the following best describes your current situation

1. Yes. I'm all fine thanks.
2. Ah, raised some good points. Got me thinking.
3. Woa. I recognise I need to take action at some point.
4. This is all too overwhelming. I need help with this – fast.
5. I'm going to focus on my top 3 priorities from the list.

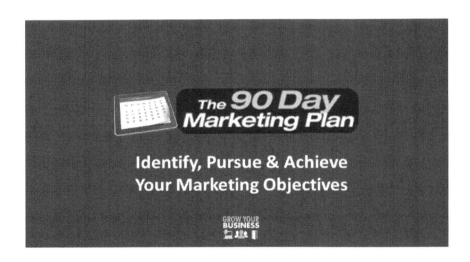

Part 4 – High Growth

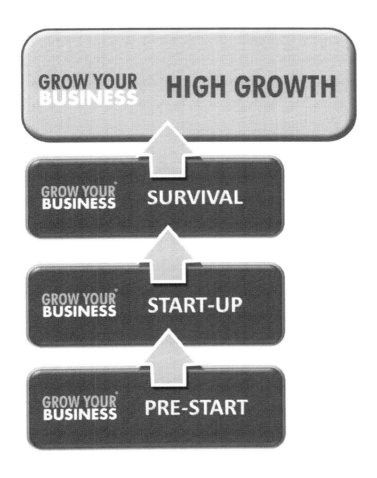

Reporting Systems

Identify what's holding you back and preventing you from growing your existing business.   Answer each of the questions below, then complete the exercise at the end of the section.

Are you ahead of your financial projections for the year to date as per your business plan?
Are you ahead of your financial projections for the quarter as per your sales plan?
Have you generated more leads and new customers for the month as per your marketing plan?

Do you know how much money you owe and to whom?
Have you updated your terms and conditions in the last 3 months?
Do you know how much is owed to you and from whom?

Do you what your monthly operating expenses and total overheads are?
Do you know if you are on the best rates with your suppliers?
Do you know what 7 words to use to get better rates with your existing suppliers?

Do you know what your most profitable revenue streams are?
Do you know what your least profitable revenue streams are?
Do you know how much extra per month you'd need to sell to achieve your financial goals?

Do you know the length of your sales cycle?
Do you know how many suspects are in your town or local postal area?
Do you which customer drains the most of your human, technical or financial resources?

Do you know what the average length of stay on your website is by visitors?

Do you know of at least 7 ways to improve your cash flow?

Do you know your most effective method for generating leads?

Do you know how many signups you're generating on a daily basis?

Do you know how many backlinks you're generating on a daily basis?

Do you know how many visitors you're generating on a daily basis?

Do you know how many NEW inbound enquiries you're generating on a MONTHLY basis?

Do you know how many NEW proposals you are sending out on a MONTHLY basis?

Do you know how many non-converted leads you have on your database or CRM?

Do you know your current cost per lead and cost per sale?

Do you know how many steps you have in your sales process?

Do you know what your closing rate is & how much you've "left on the table" in 12 months?

Do you know how much you should be charging on a day rate or hourly rate for your time?

Do you know how much revenue you NEED to be generating on a daily basis?

Do you know how many leads you need to give you the revenue you want per month?

If you were to sell your business, do you know how much you would ask for it?

If you reduced your prices by 30% how many extra sales do you need to match current profit?

If you increased your prices by 10% do you know what impact that would that line?

Do you produce a monthly Sales, P & L report or Balance sheet?

Do you monitor your inbound marketing on a monthly basis? (Calls, emails, RFI, RFPs)

Would you like a free confidential Chat to discuss your score and available options?

Add up all your NO responses & make a note of your TOTAL
Which of the following best describes your current situation

1. Yes. I'm all fine thanks.
2. Ah, raised some good points. Got me thinking.
3. Woa. I recognise I need to take action at some point.
4. This is all too overwhelming. I need help with this – fast.
5. I'm going to focus on my top 3 priorities from the list.

Leadership & Team Development

Identify what's holding you back and preventing you from growing your existing business. Answer each of the questions below, then complete the exercise at the end of the section.

Do you have a personal statement?
Do you have a personal life plan?
Are you currently participating in personal development coaching?

Do you have a Mission Statement for your business?
Do you have a Vision Statement for your business?
Do you have a Values Statement for your business?

Are your personal goals clearly defined for the year ahead?
Are your professional goals clearly defined for the year ahead?
Are your commercial goals and objectives clearly defined for the year ahead?

Have you shared your goals and objectives with your staff?
Have you shared your goals and objectives with your sales team?
Have you shared your goals and objectives with your professional advisers?

Have you created a good positive staff culture within your business?
Do you organise regular social activities for and with your staff?
Do you host regular staff meetings to identify, discuss and address key issues?

Do you ask for advice and take counsel from your professional advisers?

Do you ask for input and feedback from staff?

Do you share your thoughts, and vision with your staff regularly?

Do you allow sales staff to make key decisions?

Do you encourage sales staff to make key decisions?

Do you encourage sales staff to take on more responsibility?

Do you reward and incentivise your sales staff for demonstrating their initiative?

Do you regularly thank your sales staff for their effort & commitment to your business?

Do you have a pension, benefits or BONUS scheme in place for yourself or sales staff?

Do you invest regularly in training for yourself & staff?

Do you focus on "we" instead of "me" or "I"?

Do you do what you say you will do?

Do you lead from the front and set example of what you want others to emulate?

Do you encourage, motivate and incentivise others to execute/implement your plan?

Are you approachable and open to suggestions from others?

Do you treat others how you like to be treated?

Does each member of sales staff monitor, record and report on their progress to you?

Do you encourage sales staff and others to solve problems instead of asking you?

Do you delegate tasks effectively?

Are you looking to recruit, hire or increase the size of your team in the next 12 months?

Would you like a free confidential Chat to discuss your score & your available options?

Add up all your NO responses & make a note of your TOTAL
Which of the following best describes your current situation

1. Yes. I'm all fine thanks.
2. Ah, raised some good points. Got me thinking.
3. Woa. I recognise I need to take action at some point.
4. This is all too overwhelming. I need help with this – fast.
5. I'm going to focus on my top 3 priorities from the list.

Quality Management System

Identify what's holding you back and preventing you from growing your existing business. Answer each of the questions below, then complete the exercise at the end of the section.

Do you know what the 8 Quality Management principles are?
Are you motivated and committed to applying them in your business?
Do you have a written quality policy for your business?

Have you allocated appropriate human, technical & financial resources to your QMS?
Have you identified which certification body you will use for final assessment?
Have you already conducted a GAP Analysis & Management Review of the business?

Have you created a written plan to address the GAPS identified?
Have you identified an internal champion or team to implement your Quality Plan?
Has your plan been shared with all members of staff within your organisation?

Are senior management committed to achieving your Quality Policy?
Has Your Policy been shared with all members of staff?
Have roles & responsibilities of all staff been defined (in a chart) and communicated?

Have you produced a Quality Management System (QMS) Manual for your organisation?
Have you documented the mandatory as well as your operational procedures?
Have you ensured your QMS is designed around your business's processes?

Have all staff received the appropriate training for their roles and is it documented?
Have your internal QMS Audit staff received the appropriate "quality" training?
Are all staff aware of your QMS and know how to use it and why it is in place?

Do you have a schedule for internal audits to ensure your QMS is working correctly?
Does your internal auditing add value to the business and in assisting the management?
Can you confirm that all 8 QMS principles are being implemented across the business?

Have all procedures been developed and all instructions been written for the business?
Do you regularly conduct a management review of all aspects of your QMS?
Do you ensure that internal auditors do NOT audit their own department or work area?

Are the results of internal audits regularly reviewed by the senior management team?
Are all necessary QMS decisions being made & the appropriate actions being taken?
Have you carried out a pre-assessment audit to win trust and confidence of staff?

Do non-conformities get documented and addressed as quickly as possible?
Has a certification body been engaged for a final assessment?
PLAN – Are management reviews planned and conducted regularly?

DO – Are changes implemented on a small scale first to see the impact of the changes?

CHECK – Do you monitor processes against procedures & quality of your output?

ACT - Do you take regular action to continually improve process performance?

Are all changes in the business documented according to appropriate requirements?

Would you like a free confidential Chat to discuss your score & your available options?

Add up all your NO responses & make a note of your TOTAL
Which of the following best describes your current situation

1. Yes. I'm all fine thanks.
2. Ah, raised some good points. Got me thinking.
3. Woa. I recognise I need to take action at some point.
4. This is all too overwhelming. I need help with this – fast.
5. I'm going to focus on my top 3 priorities from the list.

Growth or EXIT?

Identify what's holding you back and preventing you from growing your existing business.   Answer each of the questions below, then complete the exercise at the end of the section.

Do you know if you want to scale, grow or EXIT your business?
Do you have a written business plan & marketing plan for the year ahead?
Do you have a quality management system (QMS) in place?

Do you meet the requirements to bid for local or central government contracts?
Do you meet the requirements to bid for larger private sector contracts?
Are you protected in the event of a legal dispute with staff?

Can your business be run day-to-day without you having to be there?
Are your policies, procedures & systems all documented?
Do you comply with (and have documented) all the necessary CSR requirements?

Do you comply with all the necessary data, privacy & security requirements?
Do you comply with all the necessary health & safety requirements?
Do you comply with all the necessary environmental requirements for your industry?

Do you have an EXIT plan for exiting within the next 5 years?
Do your shareholders, stakeholders of investors have an EXIT plan?
Are you considering Franchising/Licensing your Business or IPR in the next 5 years?

Are you planning just to have the one outlet, office or location for your business?

Are you planning to embrace mobile marketing over the next 12 months & beyond?

Are you planning to operate in more than one country?

Are you and your stakeholders satisfied with current level of sales & turnover?

Are you and your stakeholders satisfied with current level of profitability?

Are you and your stakeholders satisfied with current level of market share?

Are you satisfied with the number of product lines you have?

Are you "disruptive" in your marketplace?

Can your current customer service and support infrastructure cope with a 30% growth?

Do you require more or new funding or investment?

Do you have a source for the funding?

Do you have a repayment plan or ROI plan in place?

Are all assets & intellectual property documented, registered and protected?

Is your business and staff performing at maximum capacity?

Do you have all the reporting systems in place that you & stakeholders need or want?

Do you have the correct management team in place to help you grow your business?

Do you have the correct staff and skillsets in place to help you grow your business?

Do you have the correct equipment & technology in place to help grow your business?

Do you wish things to continue the way they are at the moment?

Have you given up in wanting to grow your business and take it to the next level?

Would you like a free confidential Chat to discuss your score & available options?

Add up all your NO responses & make a note of your TOTAL
Which of the following best describes your current situation

1. Yes. I'm all fine thanks.
2. Ah, raised some good points. Got me thinking.
3. Woa. I recognise I need to take action at some point.
4. This is all too overwhelming. I need help with this – fast.
5. I'm going to focus on my top 3 priorities from the list.

Sales Territories

Identify what's holding you back and preventing you from growing your existing business. Answer each of the questions below, then complete the exercise at the end of the section.

Have you and/or your team been trained in a specific selling "system"?
Do you have a written sales plan document?
Do you have a defined sales territory and know how many "suspects" are in it?

Do you know the value of your sales territories?
Do you know how many competitors are in each sales territory?
Do you know how much business you're losing within each sales territory?

Are you generating enough new prospects who are interested in your services?
Are you closing enough prospects, and converting enough sales/revenue?
Are you always getting sales in your territory without having to reduce your margin?

Are you and your sales team happy, motivated and achieving "targets"?
Is the business you are winning worth far more than the work it takes to fulfil?
Are you winning more business than your competitors & thus increasing your share?

Do you know how many sales reps you need to cover all your territory or territories?

Have you completed a prospect profile to target those within your territory?

Do you know how many new accounts you want to acquire within your territory?

Do you know how many accounts you need to retain with your territory?

Does 80% of your sales revenue come from 20% of your customer base within your territory?

Do you know how much revenue you need from each account to achieve your objectives?

Do you know the top 3 reasons why people do business with competitors in your territory?

Do you know the top 3 reasons are people do business with you in your territory?

Do you always track your prospecting and sales activities on a daily basis?

Do you know what the top 3 objectives are you need to achieve to grow your territory?

Do you know what the top 3 big problems are you need to address to grow your territory?

Do you have other value added items you can use to increase or reduce the price?

Do you know what upsell opportunities exist within your sales territory?

Do you know what cross-sell opportunities exist within your sales territory?

Do you have a sales recruitment, induction, or training procedure in place?

Do you have an offline prospecting plan for your sales territory?

Do you have a mobile prospecting plan for your sales territory?
Do you have an online prospecting plan for your sales territory?

Are you keeping track of the latest (and breaking) developments of all your accounts?

Do you follow your best accounts' social media channels?

Do you know what industries, sectors or niches are growing in your territory?

Have you evaluated and ranked each of your accounts within the territory?

Do you know how many accounts or prospects you can visit or contact each day?

Would you like a free confidential Chat to discuss your score & your available options?

 Add up all your NO responses & make a note of your TOTAL Which of the following best describes your current situation

1. Yes. I'm all fine thanks.
2. Ah, raised some good points. Got me thinking.
3. Woa. I recognise I need to take action at some point.
4. This is all too overwhelming. I need help with this – fast.
5. I'm going to focus on my top 3 priorities from the list.

Franchising & Licensing

Identify what's holding you back and preventing you from growing your existing business. Answer each of the questions below, then complete the exercise at the end of the section.

Do you have a written profile of the type of Licensee or Franchisee you want?

Have you decided on what the investment will be for your "opportunity"?

Have you decided on the basis for determining a Territory?

Do you know how many suspects there are in each territory?

Do you know the "value" of each territory?

Do you have a Launch plan for each territory?

Have you created a Licence / Franchise Agreement?

Have you created your Operations Manual or Licence Handbook?

Have you created a Franchise Information Memorandum and all your marketing collateral?

Do you know how many KPIs you have for holding them accountable?

Have you created your induction, training and education programmes?

Have you created template ads and scripts for them to use?

Do you know how many leads a franchisee need to create the revenue they want?

Do you know how much traffic a franchisee need to create the revenue they want?

Do you know how many referrals they need to create the revenue they want?

Have you undertaken a pilot to prove the model?
Has someone else undertaken a pilot to prove the model?
Have you got a written PR strategy document?

Have you protected your IPR?
Have you determined what IPR a franchisee will receive for their investment?
What steps have you taken in order to be able to replace the franchise in a territory?

Are you regularly featured in local, national or international press?
Are you regularly featured in trade journals/magazines for your industry?
Are you featured on any "expert" sites online?

Have you completed an offline and online competitor's analysis?
Have you completed the demand for your services in each territory?
Have you completed marketing research & a means of monitoring Franchise marketing?

Have you created a Marketing Training Programme?
Have you created a Sales Training Programme?
Have you created a Personal Development Coaching Programme?

Have you created a corporate franchisor website?
Have you created individual franchisee websites?
Have you created a corporate and franchisee social media marketing plan?

Do you wish things to continue the way they are at the moment?
Have you given up in wanting to fix your franchising problems?
Would you like a free confidential Chat to discuss your score & available options?

Add up all your NO responses & make a note of your TOTAL
Which of the following best describes your current situation

1. Yes. I'm all fine thanks.
2. Ah, raised some good points. Got me thinking.
3. Woa. I recognise I need to take action at some point.
4. This is all too overwhelming. I need help with this – fast.
5. I'm going to focus on my top 3 priorities from the list.

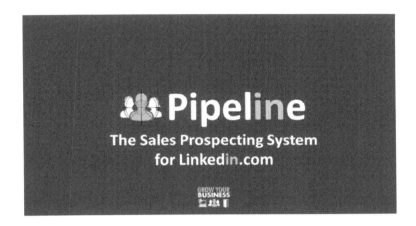

One Last Thing...

Have you found **value** and **benefit** from reading this book and in being introduced to different ideas to test with your marketing?

Do you think others struggling with marketing ideas would find a **benefit** from reading this book if they didn't know about the software solutions I share?

Would you be prepared to **recommend** my book to others, or be prepared to write a positive review about it?

Who would be the first two people that you know who are self-employed or running their own business, that might benefit from reading this kindle book too?

I really hope you have got value from my book. You definitely will if you choose to take action, and start making changes to your marketing approach with the ideas I've shared.

Take a moment, reflect on this book and write down the top 5 key "takeaways" you've gained from this book. Write what you've learned and consider adding a review of the book, for amazing things are about to start happening when you begin embracing and applying the principles contained herein, and my other books.

In addition to adding a review, consider sharing your thoughts via your online networks such as Linkedin, Facebook and twitter. If you believe the book is worth sharing, please would you take a few seconds to let your friends know about it? If it turns out to make a difference in their lives and businesses, they'll be forever grateful to you, as will I.

You can add your review by revisiting our product page in the Amazon Kindle Store.

About The Author

Unlike other business coaches, social media & marketing consultants I approach my marketing coaching and consultancy from a refreshing perspective of wanting to be held accountable to generate confidence, progress & results...

...without offering prescriptive advice.

• My latest book is called "Entrepreneurship & The Entrepreneurial Journey"
• All 16 previous books got to #1 for their category on Amazon
• Pulled over 250,000 views to a blog in 24 hrs
• Generated as much as 236 leads on Linkedin in 24 hrs

Can I help you?
Maybe. Maybe Not.

YES, IF YOU WANT HELP TO:

• Raise your profile online
• Document & Execute a NEW Marketing Strategy
• Hold your marketing staff, agency or VA accountable
• Fill Your Sales Funnel, Sales Pipeline with NEW leads
• Get GDPR ready & Grow Your Business®

If any of the above describe your current situation then imagine a few weeks from now, experiencing the positive, permanent breakthroughs you or your stakeholders want.

Many small business owners are struggling to justify allocating human, technical or financial resources to grow their business without it translating into NEW leads, sales and revenue.

That's where I come in.

After all, Knowledge is NOT power. Applied knowledge is.

SOME QUICK FACTS

• Creator of the Pipeline Sales Prospecting System
• Author of "The Lead Generation MBA" Course
• Been featured on TV - twice.
• Over 400 testimonials on the UKs oldest social network
• A former Scottish & UK Shell Livewire, Royal Bank of Scotland & PSYBT Winner

I WORK WITH

• Entrepreneurs
• Business Owners
• C Level Managers
• Board Members

of

• Pre-start
• Start-up
• Small
• High Growth Businesses

In addition to business coaching, I can also assist you in EXECUTING a measurable, practical plan of action with full accountability & no excuses - ever.

I am also available for Keynote speeches, workshops, webinars and as a guest Panellist.

Explore my Linkedin profile. Claim your FREE "Instant Breakthrough" & to discuss your score, call me on +44 (0)1542 841319, SKYPE me (Pocketmentor) or ping me via Linkedin.

My Linkedin Profile –
www.fraserhay.co.uk

Other Work by the Author

For more, visit: www.fraserhay.com

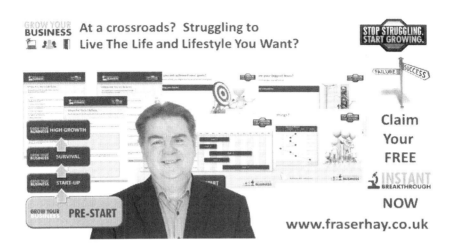

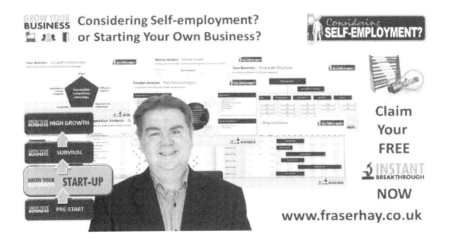

Visit www.fraserhay.co.uk today & Claim Your FREE "Instant Breakthrough"

Visit www.fraserhay.co.uk today & Claim Your FREE "Instant Breakthrough"

Printed in Great Britain
by Amazon